TREASURES OF THE

MUSEUM OF FINE ARTS

BOSTON

TREASURES OF THE

MUSEUM OF FINE ARTS

BOSTON

INTRODUCTION BY MALCOLM ROGERS

CHAPTER INTRODUCTIONS BY GILIAN WOHLAUER

A TINY FOLIO™
ABBEVILLE PRESS   PUBLISHERS
NEW YORK   LONDON   PARIS

Front cover: Detail of Pierre-Auguste Renoir, *Dance at Bougival,* 1883.
See page 235.

Back cover: John Singer Sargent, *The Daughters of Edward D. Boit,* 1882.
See page 153.

Spine: Paul Revere II, *Teapot.* Boston, c. 1760–65. See page 125.

Frontispiece: Detail of Vincent van Gogh, *Postman Joseph Roulin,* 1888.
See page 255.

Page 6: View of the grand staircase at the Museum of Fine Arts, Boston.

Page 16: Detail of *Pair Statue of King Mycerinus and His Queen,* Egypt (Giza),
c. 2548–2530 B.C. (4th dynasty). See page 21.

Page 162: Detail of *Christ in Majesty with Symbols of the Four Evangelists;
The Apostles with Scenes from the Story of Cain and Abel; and Scenes from the Life
of Christ.* Spanish (Catalan), 12th century. See page 170.

Page 222: Detail of Claude Monet, *Water Lilies (II),* 1907. See page 243.

Page 258: Detail of Pablo Picasso, *Rape of the Sabine Women,* 1963. See page 287.

For copyright and Cataloging-in-Publication Data, see page 319.

CONTENTS

INTRODUCTION

The Museum of Fine Arts, Boston, is one of the greatest encyclopedic museums in the world. It was also one of the first to be founded in America. Its outstanding and, in some cases, unequaled collections of some 750,000 objects include American and European decorative arts and sculpture; Asian, Ancient Egyptian, Nubian, Near Eastern, African, Oceanic, Pre-Columbian, and Classical art; musical instruments; American and European paintings, prints, drawings, and photographs; textiles and costumes; and contemporary art. The Museum has a renowned art school, the School of the Museum of Fine Arts, and is also an active partner with the Museum of the National Center for Afro-American Arts in Roxbury, Massachusetts. Throughout the Museum's 125 years, it has welcomed more than 51 million visitors from around the world who have come to enjoy and learn from these remarkable collections. These treasures are displayed in distinguished and beautiful exhibition galleries, housed in a handsome Classical Revival building that dates from the early years of the twentieth century.

The Museum of Fine Arts was founded on February 4, 1870, when the Massachusetts legislature passed an act establishing a board of trustees "for the purpose of erecting a museum for the preservation and exhibition of works of art, of making, maintaining, and establishing collections of such works, and of affording instruction in the Fine Arts." Less than four months after the incorporation of the Museum, the city of Boston awarded the MFA a tract of land that faced what was later to become Copley Square. The 91,000-square-foot lot was granted to the trustees on the condition that they erect upon it, within three years, a building costing $100,000. A committee was appointed to solicit funds for construction, and they moved forward with such energy that before the summer of 1871, nearly $250,000 had been pledged. The trustees chose architects John H. Sturgis and Charles Brigham's plan of a red brick and terra-cotta gothic structure for the Museum, which opened to the public on July 4, 1876. The trustees then raised $126,000 to complete the facade and the East Wing, which opened on July 1, 1879. The building would be expanded again in 1890.

In 1899, deeming it the proper time to plan for new and enlarged facilities, the trustees purchased land on Huntington Avenue, approximately one mile from the Copley Square location. Construction of the present granite building, from designs by the Boston architect Guy Lowell, commenced in 1907, and the Museum of Fine Arts reopened in 1909. From the planning stages of the Huntington Avenue museum it had been hoped that contemporary artists would

Cyrus Edwin Dallin (1861–1944).
Appeal to the Great Spirit, 1909.
Bronze, height: 122 in. (309.9 cm).

adorn the building and grounds with their works. In 1913 the well-known bronze equestrian statue *Appeal to the Great Spirit* (page 9) by Cyrus Edwin Dallin became the centerpiece of the forecourt of the Museum.

The new building was financed entirely by private individuals, led by the trustees. Shortly after its opening, Mrs. Robert Dawson Evans contributed an extraordinarily generous gift of one million dollars, in her husband's memory, to provide a new wing. The Evans Wing opened in 1915 and offered a 40 percent increase in exhibition space. Since then, the building has continued to grow, with expansions in 1928, 1967, 1969, 1970, and 1981, with the opening of the new West Wing designed by I. M. Pei. This exciting space houses the Museum's shop, restaurants, auditorium, and largest special exhibition space, the Graham Gund Gallery.

The Department of Education (established in 1942) fulfills the Museum's mission "to serve a wide variety of people through direct encounters with works of art." Twenty percent of all visitors come to the Museum to attend education programs. The department organizes lectures, seminars, art classes, concerts, and film screenings on almost every day of the year. The education department greatly enhances the Museum's reputation as a valued resource for the New England community and beyond.

The Museum of Fine Arts presents some eighteen stimulating temporary exhibitions and collection rotations each year. In addition, there are reinstallations of permanent displays and a nationally famous flower festival—Art in Bloom—which is celebrated each spring. The Museum is constantly growing and changing. For instance, the Helen and Richard Fraser Garden Court reopened to the public in April 1996. This European garden, with its statues and fountains, dates from 1928 and is located in the heart of the Museum. There are two additional gardens, the West Courtyard Garden and the Japanese Garden, Tenshin-en, or "The Garden of the Heart of Heaven." These beautiful green spaces flourish three seasons of the year, providing our visitors with a pleasant retreat and the perfect complement to the Museum's varied displays.

Throughout the years, generous donors have not only enriched the Museum's collections, they have also provided endowment funds. The Museum, founded as a private institution, still receives virtually no government funding for its operations. Only a few of the many contributors can be mentioned in this brief introduction. The Museum's Asian collection, considered one of the finest in America and the most comprehensive under one roof in the world, was formed primarily through the munificence of Edward Sylvester Morse, William Sturgis Bigelow, Ernest Fenollosa, Charles Goddard Weld, Ananda

Coomaraswamy, and Denman Waldo Ross. Morse, a zoologist, traveled to Japan in 1877 to collect marine brachiopods. Once there, he became fascinated with Japanese ceramics and formed a collection of approximately six thousand pieces. Morse then encouraged Fenollosa and Bigelow to visit Japan. These men of great vision formed superb collections of Japanese art, which they brought to the Museum of Fine Arts on their return to the city. Their contributions began the Museum's outstanding Asian collection, which now includes works of art from Turkey to the Far East.

The tastes of these important Bostonians also shaped the character of the Museum's collection of paintings, which has grown to be one of the foremost in the world, with works ranging in date from the eleventh to the twentieth century. Boston collectors were among the first to appreciate the revolutionary developments of nineteenth-century French art, and the Museum has unparalleled holdings of nearly seventy paintings and pastels by Jean-François Millet. Works by the Impressionists—especially Claude Monet, Edouard Manet, Camille Pissarro, Alfred Sisley, and Pierre-Auguste Renoir—were eagerly sought by Bostonians and donated to the Museum, and now form a high point of any visitor's tour.

The collection of American art is one of the finest in the country. This city of historic and cultural tradition has provided the Museum of Fine Arts with a spectacular panorama of painting in eighteenth- and nineteenth-century America. Particularly significant are the Museum's Colonial and Federal portraits, dominated by more than sixty works by John Singleton Copley, and the M. and M. Karolik Collection of American Paintings from 1815 to 1865, as well as the donation, also from the Karoliks, of some three thousand American drawings that span the nineteenth century.

In 1928 the Museum of Fine Arts built a new decorative arts wing to house the American and European holdings and several furnished period rooms. The collection is exceptionally strong in the period of pre–Civil War New England. The collection of European decorative arts and sculpture includes comprehensive holdings of English silver and porcelain as well as a marvelous group of French silver, the bequest of Elizabeth Parke and Harvey S. Firestone, Jr. In addition, there are fine collections of medieval art, fascinating and rare musical instruments, and a preeminent collection of textiles and costumes. In 1870 Boston was the center of the United States textile industry, and the Museum's founders set out to form a collection to provide access to examples of good design. In 1890 Denman Waldo Ross, Harvard professor of design and a Museum of Fine Arts trustee, established the collection with his gifts of Coptic and Andean textiles;

European, Turkish, Indian, and Persian silk weavings; Indonesian batiks; and Middle Eastern rugs. These splendid textiles can be seen in changing exhibitions in the Museum's Textile Gallery and Tapestry Gallery.

The Museum's Classical holdings, including Greek, Roman, and Etruscan art, are equally impressive. The Museum acquired its first Classical antiquities in 1872, when a group of objects from Cyprus was purchased from General di Cesnola. The major part of the collection was formed between 1890 and 1910; during this period more than four thousand objects entered the Museum. The pursuit of many of these objects was the work of one man, Edward Perry Warren, the Museum's agent in the acquisition of Classical antiquities. Purchased by the trustees, these objects, many of remarkable quality, form the nucleus of the Museum's classical holdings. They stand today as a monument to Warren's taste and connoisseurship.

Unlike the Museum's other collections, that of ancient Egyptian, Nubian, and Near Eastern art was formed largely as a result of scientific excavations. In 1905 the Museum of Fine Arts joined with Harvard University to form an expedition in Egypt based at the Pyramids of Giza under the direction of curator Dr. George Andrew Reisner. Over the forty-year duration of this expedition, the Museum acquired, through the share of antiquities assigned to it by the Egyptian government, exceptionally beautiful and significant Old Kingdom sculptures, a group unparalleled outside Cairo.

In 1971 the youngest of the Museum's departments was formed: the Contemporary Art department, which includes art in all media by artists who have emerged since 1955. Abstract paintings constitute an important part of its holdings, including major canvases by Morris Louis and paintings by Helen Frankenthaler and Kenneth Noland.

The Museum's collection of prints, drawings, and photographs is one of the world's greatest resources. It consists of approximately three hundred thousand prints, drawings, watercolors, illustrated books, posters, and photographs of American and European origin dating from the mid-fifteenth century to the present day. The Objects Conservation and Scientific Research Laboratory and other Museum conservation laboratories for furniture, paper, paintings, and Asian paintings are also centers for scientific study and analysis, providing care for the Museum's varied collections.

This book provides a tour of just a sampling of the very many treasures housed within the walls of the Museum of Fine Arts, Boston, some of which, due to their fragile nature, can be exhibited only occasionally. The goal of this volume parallels that of the Museum as a whole: to encourage inquiry and to heighten understanding and appreciation of the visual arts.

Malcolm Rogers
Ann and Graham Gund Director

THE ANCIENT WORLD

Some of the most exciting works of art in the Museum are those that take us farthest back in time; they came into the collection not only through gifts and purchases but also from archaeological excavations. The world-famous collection of ancient Egyptian art was begun in 1905, when the Museum joined Harvard University in an archaeological expedition under the direction of Dr. George Andrew Reisner. The expedition, based at the Great Pyramids at Giza, continued for forty years. The Museum's share of the antiquities excavated during this expedition brought to Boston a group of Old Kingdom sculptures equaled only in Cairo. One masterpiece is the noble and intimate statue of Mycerinus, builder of the Third Pyramid at Giza, and his queen (at left and page 21). Other great treasures are the miraculously preserved painted coffin from Bersheh in Upper Egypt and the carved and painted procession of offering bearers—at once timeless and evocatively immediate—from the same tomb (page 25).

Dr. Reisner also directed excavations in the Sudan that brought to the Museum a collection of Nubian art matched only in Khartoum; highlights include colossal sculptures of ancient Nubian kings, dazzling gold jewelry, finely crafted ceramics, and one of the largest granite sarcophagi ever excavated. With excavations renewed in 1986 at the site of Gebel Barkal, the Museum continues to contribute to ongoing exploration of Nubian history and culture.

Also from the ancient world is a small but distinguished Near Eastern collection of sculpture, bronzes, cylinder seals, and other objects from Mesopotamia, the Syrian coast, Anatolia, and Persia. A major example is the monumental stone relief from Nimrud in Assyria, carved with muscular guardian figures designed to protect the king (page 39).

The holdings of Greek, Roman, and Etruscan art contain many objects of outstanding quality, including the delicate ivory-and-gold female figure entwined with snakes (page 45), one of very few sculptures in ivory to survive from the fabled Minoan civilization of Crete. The collection of Greek vases is very strong; such red-figure examples as the krater with intricate and energized images of the fall of Troy (page 56) provide a comprehensive survey of the work of the major painters of fifth-century Athens. Also from the Classical period of Greek art is the serene marble head of Aphrodite, goddess of love (page 62), which is very close in style and craftsmanship to sculpture by the great Praxiteles. An exquisitely fashioned gold earring—a tiny figure of Nike driving her chariot (page 51)—was most likely created as a dedication to a goddess and may have been worn by a statue. Another strength of the collection is the excellent group of Græco-Roman and Roman marble portrait busts, which ranges from the powerfully naturalistic head of the aged, blind Homer (page 69) to the sensitive but idealized likeness of the first Roman emperor, Augustus, who was revered as a god after his death (page 67).

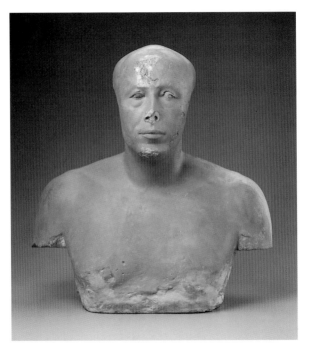

Bust of Vizier Ankh-haf.
Egypt (Giza), c. 2625–2600 B.C. (4th dynasty).
Painted limestone, height: 21 in. (53.3 cm).

Pair Statue of King Mycerinus and His Queen.
Egypt (Giza), c. 2548–2530 B.C. (4th dynasty).
Graywacke, height: 54½ in. (140 cm).

Triad of King Mycerinus and Two Goddesses.
Egypt (Giza), c. 2548–2530 B.C. (4th dynasty).
Graywacke, height: 32⅞ in. (83.5 cm).

Statue of the Lady Sennuwy.
Egypt (found at Kerma, Sudan), c. 1950 B.C. (12th dynasty).
Black granite, height: 67¾ in. (172 cm).

Statue of Wepwawet-em-hat.
Egypt (Asyut), c. 2230–2060 B.C. (First Intermediate period).
Painted wood, height: 44⅛ in. (112 cm).

Procession of Priest and Offering Bearers.
Egypt (Bersheh), c. 2000 B.C. (11th dynasty).
Painted wood, height: 17⅜ in. (44 cm).

Mummy Mask.
Egypt, 1st half of 1st century A.D. (Early Roman period).
Painted and gilded cartonnage with inlaid glass,
22½ x 11½ x 13¾ in. (57.2 x 29.2 x 35 cm).

Mummy Case of Ta-bes.
Egypt, c. 946–712 B.C. (22d dynasty).
Painted cartonnage, 59 x 11¾ in. (150 x 30 cm).

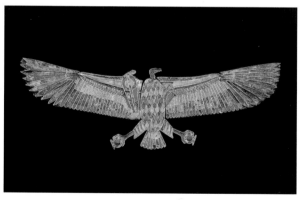

Pectoral.
Egypt, c. 1750–1570 B.C. (Second Intermediate period).
Silver, electrum, and gold with inlays of carnelian and glass,
14⅜ x 4⅜ in. (36.5 x 11.2 cm).

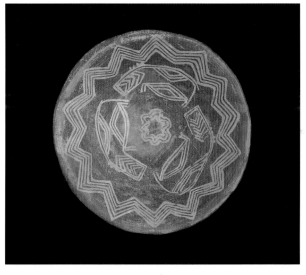

Bowl.
Egypt, c. 3500 B.C. (Predynastic).
Pottery, diameter: 7½ in. (19.1 cm).

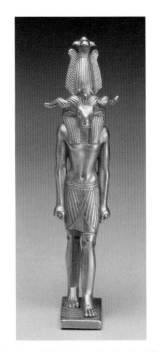

*Amulet of God Harsaphes Inscribed for
King Neferkare of Heracleopolis.*
Egypt (Ehnasya), c. 750–720 B.C. (23d dynasty).
Gold, height: 2⅜ in. (6 cm).

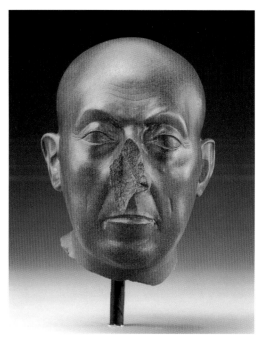

Portrait of a Man: "The Boston Green Head."
Egypt, 3d century B.C. (Ptolemaic period).
Green schist, height: 4⅛ in. (10.5 cm).

Mirror of Shabaka, King of Egypt and Kush.
Nubia (el-Kurru, Sudan), c. 716–701 B.C. (25th dynasty).
Bronze with gilt-silver handle, height: 13 in. (32.9 cm).

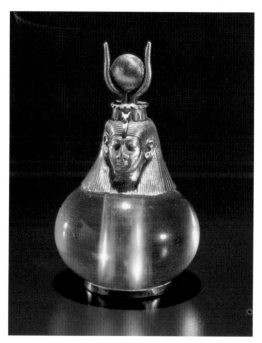

Spherical Amulet with the Head of the Goddess Hathor.
Nubia (el-Kurru, Sudan), from the tomb of a queen of Piye,
King of Kush, c. 747–716 B.C. (25th dynasty).
Rock crystal and gold, height: 2⅛ in. (5.3 cm).

Statue of Aspelta, King of Kush.
Nubia (Gebel Barkal, Sudan), c. 600–580 B.C.
(Napatan period). Black granite, once partially gilded,
height: 130¾ in. (332 cm).

Shawabtis (Funerary Figures) of Taharqa, King of Egypt and Kush.
Nubia (Nuri, Sudan), c. 690–664 B.C.
Granite, serpentine, and calcite, height: varies,
3⅞–19⅝ in. (10–50 cm).

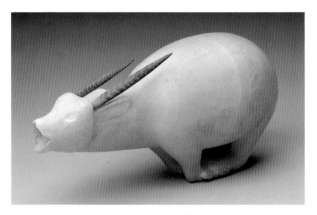

Perfume Vessel in the Shape of a Bound Oryx.
Nubia (Meroë, Sudan), early 7th century B.C. (25th dynasty).
Calcite, horns restored,
6¾ x 3¼ x 2⅜ in. (17.2 x 8.3 x 6.1 cm).

Bracelet.
Nubia (Gebel Barkal, Sudan), from the tomb of a ruling
queen of Kush, 2d century B.C. (Meroitic period).
Gold and enamel, open: ¾ x 4⅞ in. (1.8 x 12.5 cm).   37

Relief from the Ishtar Gate.
Babylon (Iraq), reign of Nebuchadnezzar II,
604–562 B.C. (Neo-Babylonian period).
Glazed brick, 40⅛ x 91¾ in. (102 x 233 cm).

Relief of a Winged Deity.
Iraq, from the Northwest Palace at Nimrud, Assyria,
reign of Ashurnasirpal II, c. 883–859 B.C. (Neo-Assyrian
period). Alabaster, 90½ x 68½ in. (230 x 174 cm).   39

Horse Collar with Winged Sphinxes.
Eastern Anatolia (Urartu), 7th century B.C.
Bronze, 13 x 23 x 2½ in. (33 x 58.4 x 6.4 cm).

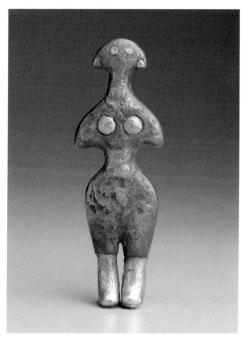

Figurine of a Goddess.
Central Anatolia (Alaca Hüyük?), c. 2500–2300 B.C.
(Early Bronze Age II period).
Silver with gold inlays, height: 4¼ in. (10.8 cm).

Plate with Mountain Goat.
Iran, c. A.D. 224–651 (Sasanian period).
Silver with details mercury gilded, diameter: 8⅜ in. (21.2 cm).

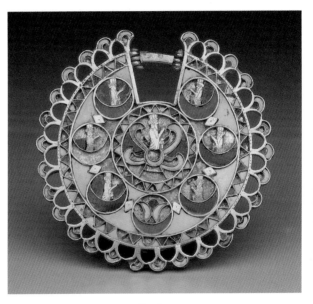

Earring.
Iran, c. 525–330 B.C. (Achaemenid period).
Gold cloisonné with inlays of turquoise, lapis lazuli,
and carnelian, diameter: 2 in. (5 cm).   43

Votive Double Ax.
Crete, c. 1500 B.C. (Late Minoan period, Bronze Age).
Gold, 3½ x 3¼ in. (9 x 8.3 cm).

Woman Holding Snakes.
Crete, c. 1600–1500 B.C. (Late Minoan period, Bronze Age).
Ivory and gold, height: 6⅜ in. (16.1 cm).

Deer Nursing Her Fawn.
Thebes (central Greece), 8th century B.C. (Geometric period).
Bronze, height: 2⅞ in. (7.2 cm).

Apollo, Dedicated by Mantiklos.
Boeotia (central Greece), c. 700 B.C. (Late Geometric or Early
Orientalizing period). Bronze, height: 8 in. (20.3 cm).

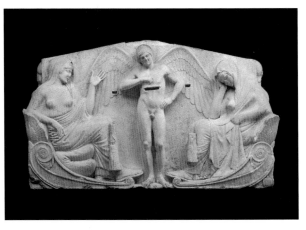

Three-Sided Relief, "Boston Throne."
South Italian Greek, c. 450 B.C. (Early Classical period).
Marble, height: 37¾ in. (96 cm).

Herakles with Club and Lion Skin.
A.D. 120–170 (Middle Roman Imperial period),
based on a 5th-century B.C. Greek prototype.
Marble, height: 22½ in. (57 cm).

Dancer.
Etruscan, c. 500 B.C. (Late Archaic period).
Bronze, height: 5¼ in. (13.4 cm).

Earring, Nike Driving a Chariot.
Found in the Peloponnesus (southern Greece), c. 350–325 B.C.
(Late Classical period). Gold, height: 2 in. (5 cm).

Black-Figure Amphora with Dionysus and Satyrs in a Vineyard.
Athenian, c. 540 B.C. (Archaic period).
Ceramic, height: 20½ in. (52 cm).

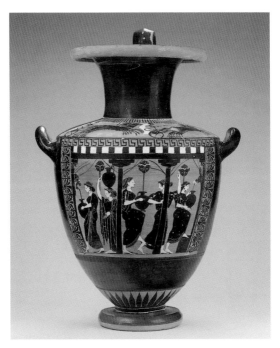

Black-Figure Hydria with Five Women at a Fountain House.
Athenian, c. 520 B.C. (Archaic period).
Ceramic, height: 20⅞ in. (53 cm).

Seated Sphinx: Upper Part of a Grave Stele.
Athenian, c. 535–530 B.C. (Archaic period).
Marble, height of sphinx: 29⅝ in. (75.2 cm),
height of support: 26⅛ in. (66.5 cm).

PAN PAINTER.
Red-Figure Krater with Pan Pursuing a Shepherd.
Athenian, c. 470 B.C. (Early Classical period).
Ceramic, height: 14⅝ in. (37 cm).

ALTAMURA PAINTER.
Red-Figure Krater with the Fall of Troy.
Athenian, c. 465 B.C. (Early Classical period).
Ceramic, height: 18⅞ in. (48 cm).

LYKAON PAINTER.
Red-Figure Pelike with Odysseus, Hermes, and Odysseus's
Companion, Elpenor, Emerging from the Underworld.
Athenian, 440 B.C. (Classical period).
Ceramic; height: 18⅝ in. (47.4 cm).

Portrait of a Woman.
A.D. 100–125 (Roman Imperial, Trajanic, or
Early Hadrianic period). Marble, height: 13¾ in. (35 cm).

Mosaic Bowl.
Alexandria or Italy, late 1st century B.C. or 1st century A.D.
(Early Roman Imperial period). Pillar-molded blue and
white glass, diameter: 4¼ in. (10.8 cm).　59

Sarcophagus with Figures of Man and Wife on the Lid.
Etruscan, 3d century B.C. (Early Hellenistic period).
Peperino, 34⅝ x 29⅞ x 82⅝ in. (88 x 76 x 210 cm).

Artemis with Bow.
Found in Mazi, near Olympia, c. 525 B.C. (Archaic period).
Bronze, height: 7½ in. (19.2 cm).

Aphrodite: "The Bartlett Head."
Athenian, c. 325–300 B.C. (Late Classical or Early
Hellenistic period). Marble, height: 11⅜ in. (28.8 cm).

Head of Zeus.
Greek (found near Milas, southwest Turkey), 4th century B.C.
(Late Classical period). Marble, height: 18⅞ in. (48 cm).

Herm of the Playwright Menander.
Found near Torre Annunziata, on Bay of Naples, c. 50–20 B.C.
(Late Republican or Early Roman Imperial period).
Marble, height: 20¼ in. (51.5 cm).

Maiden or Youthful Goddess.
Greece (found on Chios), c. 300 B.C.
(Early Hellenistic period). Marble, height: 14⅛ in. (36 cm).

Bust of the Emperor Elagabalus.
A.D. 218–222 (Roman Imperial, Late Severan period).
Marble, height: 28 in. (71 cm).

Head of the Emperor Augustus.
Found at Ariccia, near Rome, c. A.D. 40 (Early Roman
Imperial period). Marble, height: 16⅞ in. (43 cm).

Black-Figure Hydria with Achilles Dragging the Body of Hector around the Walls of Troy.
Athenian, c. 530–510 B.C. (Archaic period).
Ceramic, height: 22¼ in. (56.6 cm).

Head of the Poet Homer.
c. A.D. 50–150 (Roman Imperial period), based on a
Hellenistic Greek prototype. Marble, height: 16⅛ in. (41 cm).

ART OF ASIA

In all of the Western world, the collections of Asian art at the Museum of Fine Arts are unrivaled in size, scope, and distinction. They include paintings, prints, sculptures, textiles, ceramics, metalwork, and an abundance of decorative objects from every part of Asia, dating from the dawn of civilization to the present day.

Many adventurous nineteenth-century Bostonians were passionately interested in Asia, and the Museum's preeminent collection of Japanese art was substantially formed well before 1900, at a time when its acquisitions of American and European art had only begun. In 1877, when Boston zoologist Edward Sylvester Morse went to Japan to collect brachiopods, a species of marine invertebrate, he became fascinated with Japanese ceramics. The next year, Morse's friend Ernest Fenollosa accepted a teaching position in Tokyo, where he, too, fell under the spell of Japanese art. Fenollosa collected paintings, supported struggling artists, and urged the Japanese to preserve their extraordinary cultural heritage. In 1882 Boston physician William Sturgis Bigelow accompanied Morse and Fenollosa to Japan; Bigelow stayed for seven years, studied Buddhism, and acquired some sixty thousand works of art. The collections of Morse, Fenollosa, and

Bigelow all came to the Museum of Fine Arts. They include some of the Museum's greatest treasures, such as *Night Attack on the Sanjō Palace,* a vibrant and energetic handscroll that Fenollosa acquired about 1884 (page 79).

In addition to religious and secular painting from virtually every period and school, the Japanese collection contains a wealth of Buddhist sculpture, swords and sword fittings, ceramics, elegant robes worn by actors in the Nō theater (the finest assemblage outside Japan), and wood-block prints (more than fifty thousand examples, unparalleled in their artistic quality and superior state of preservation).

Although the Japanese collection was established first, the Museum's Asian holdings have expanded in many directions. Its Chinese art is especially rich in early ceramics and in such rare paintings as Emperor Huizong's master-piece, *Five-Colored Parakeet on Blossoming Apricot Tree,* enhanced by his elegantly written poem (page 91). Other highlights are an extensive group of Buddhist and Daoist sculptures, sumptuous lacquer objects inlaid with mother-of-pearl, and other decorative arts in bronze, jade, and glass.

The collection of Indian art (one of the first in America) was established early in the twentieth century through the collaboration of a pioneering scholar, Ananda Coomaraswamy, and a generous benefactor, Denman Waldo Ross. Among its greatest strengths are vivid, meticulously detailed Mughal and Rajput paintings and a superb group of early sculptures, including the sensuous sandstone torso of a fertility goddess from a gateway of the Great Stupa at Sanchi, one of the oldest surviving Buddhist monuments (page 99).

The Museum's Asian galleries contain arts of Korea (unusual in Western museums), painting and sculpture from Tibet and Nepal, and a fine collection of rare works from Cambodia and Indonesia. From Islamic countries, including Egypt, Iran, Iraq, and Turkey, come manuscripts, courtly paintings, metalwork, and ceramics. One of the Museum's most important textiles is a silk carpet woven with images of hunting and feasting, a masterpiece from the royal workshops of sixteenth-century Persia (page 106).

Although the Asian holdings continue to grow, the Museum's focus is now primarily on conservation, exhibition, and research. This will ensure that these great collections are preserved and remain accessible to visitors and scholars from around the world.

ON PAGE 70: ATTRIBUTED TO EMPEROR HUIZONG
(r. 1101–25, d. 1135)
Court Ladies Preparing Newly Woven Silk (detail).
China, early 12th century (Northern Song dynasty).
Handscroll; ink, color, and gold on silk,
14⅝ x 57¼ in. (37 x 145.3 cm).

The Historical Buddha Preaching on the Vulture Peak.
Japan, 8th century (Nara period). Panel; ink, color, and gold
on bast fabric, 48½ x 56½ in. (107.1 x 143.5 cm).

KAIKEI (active c. 1185–after 1220).
The Bodhisattva of the Future. Japan, 1189 (Kamakura period).
Joined woodblock construction, gilt cypress with inlaid
crystal eyes, height: 42 in. (106.6 cm).

Illustrated Handscroll of Minister Kibi's Adventures in China (detail).
Japan, late 12th century (Heian period).
Set of four handscrolls; ink, color, and gold on paper,
12⅝ in. x 80 ft. 1 in. (32 cm x 24.42 m).

The Divine Guardian of the North with His Retinue (detail).
Japan, late 12th century (Kamakura period). Panel; ink, color,
and gold on silk, 74⅞ x 26¾ in. (90.1 x 68.1 cm).

SAICHI (active mid-13th century).
The Bodhisattva of Compassion Bearing a Lotus.
Japan, 1269 (Kamakura period).
Bronze with gilding, height: 41⅞ in. (106.5 cm).

Night Attack on the Sanjō Palace (detail), from the *Illustrated Handscrolls of the Events of the Heiji Era.* Japan, 13th century (Kamakura period). Handscroll; ink and color on paper, 1 ft. 4 in. x 23 ft. (41 cm. x 7 m). 79

BUNSEI (active mid–15th century).
Landscape. Japan, late 15th century (Muromachi period).
Hanging scroll; ink and light color on paper,
28⅞ x 13 in. (73.2 x 33 cm).

SOGA SHŌHAKU (1730–1781).
The Four Sages of Mount Shang (detail). Japan, 18th century
(Edo period). Pair of six-panel folding screens; ink and gold
on paper, each 5 ft. 1 in. x 12 ft. (1.56 x 3.67 m).   81

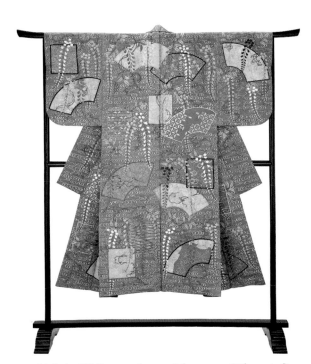

Nuihaku Nō Costume. Japan, 18th century (Edo period). Silk twill weave, embroidered with silk and stenciled with gold leaf, 59½ x 55½ in. (151 x 141 cm).

松本米三郎

東洲齋寫樂画

TŌSHŪSAI SHARAKU (active c. 1795).
*The Actor Matsumoto Yonesaburō as the Courtesan Okaru in the
Play "Chūshingura."* Japan (Edo period). Woodblock print; ink,
color, and mica on paper, 14⅝ x 9⅞ in. (37.2 x 25.1 cm). 83

Ewer and Basin.
Korea, 11th–12th century (Koryo period). Silver gilt, height
of ewer: 13 in. (33 cm), height of basin: 6¾ in. (17 cm).

Vase.
Korea, 12th century (Koryo period). Celadon stoneware
with black and white inlays, height: 12¼ in. (31 cm).

Sākyamuni Buddha Expounding the Law.
Korea, 13th century (Koryo period).
Ink and color on hemp, 65 x 33½ in. (165 x 85 cm).

Figure of a Standing Youth.
China, late 5th–early 4th century B.C. (Warring States period).
Cast bronze and carved jade, height: 11¾ in. (30 cm).

Altarpiece with Amitābha and Attendants.
China, A.D. 593 (Sui dynasty).
Cast bronze, height: 30⅛ in. (76.5 cm).

ATTRIBUTED TO YAN LIBEN (d. 673).
The Thirteen Emperors (section).
China, 7th century (Tang dynasty). Handscroll;
ink and color on silk, 1 ft. 8 in. x 17 ft. 5 in. (0.51 x 5.31 m). 89

Bodhisattva of Compassion (Guanyin).
China, 12th century (Jin dynasty). Lacquered wood with
painting and gilding, height: 55½ in. (141 cm).

EMPEROR HUIZONG (r. 1101–1125, d. 1135).
Five-Colored Parakeet on Blossoming Apricot Tree.
China, c. 1110 (Northern Song dynasty). Handscroll;
ink and color on silk, 21 x 49¼ in. (53.3 x 125.1 cm). 91

Fish.
China, 13th century (Southern Song dynasty).
Album leaf, silk tapestry (*kesi*), 9⅞ x 9⅞ in. (25 x 25 cm).

Two-tiered Stand.
China, early 16th century (Ming dynasty). Lacquered wood
with mother-of-pearl inlay, height: 18 in. (45.7 cm).

Bhairava, or Mahākāla.
Indonesia, Eastern Java, c. 14th century.
Andesite, height: 78 in. (198.1 cm).

Incense Burner with Dragon Handle and Phoenix Cover.
Vietnam, Dongson culture, 3d century A.D.
Cast bronze, 5⅜ x 7½ in. (13.5 x 19 cm).

Female Deity.
Cambodia, late 10th–early 11th century.
Bronze, height: 24¾ in. (62.9 cm).

Buddha of Eternal Life (Amitāyus).
Nepal, c. early 13th century.
Colors on cotton, 16¼ x 13 in. (41.3 x 33 cm).

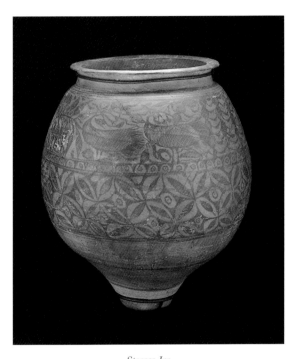

Storage Jar.
Pakistan, Chanhu-Daro, c. 2600–2100 B.C. Clay with black
decoration on red slip, height: 22¼ in. (55.3 cm).

Torso of Fertility Goddess (Yakshi).
Northern India, Madhya Pradesh, Sanchi, Stupa no. 1,
c. A.D. 25. Sandstone, height: 28⅜ in. (72 cm).

Shiva the Everlasting (Sadāśiva).
Southern India, Tamil Nadu, c. late 10th century.
Granulite, height: 64 in. (162.5 cm).

Ganesha with His Wives.
Probably central India, c. 1000–1050.
Sandstone, height: 41½ in. (105 cm).

ATTRIBUTED TO MANŌHAR.
Darbar of Jahāngīr, from a manuscript of the *Jahāngīr-nāma.*
Northern India, c. 1620 (Mughal period). Opaque watercolor
on paper, 13⅝ x 7⅝ in. (34.5 x 19.5 cm).

Lady at Her Toilette.
Northern India, Punjab Hills, Basohli, 1690–1700.
Opaque watercolor on paper, 8⅞ x 4⅝ in. (22.4 x 11.9 cm).

Pechhavai with Gopīs, Cows, and Heavenly Beings.
India, Rajasthan (Jodhpur or Bikaner), late 18th century.
Painted cotton, plain weave, 96⅛ x 100 in. (244 x 254 cm).

Alexander Fights the Monster of Habash (Ethiopia),
from a manuscript of the *Shāhnāma*.
Iran, c. 1328–36 (Ilkhānid period).
Opaque watercolor on paper, 23¼ x 15⅝ in. (59 x 39.6 cm). 105

PROBABLY DESIGNED BY AQĀ MĪRAK AND SULTĀN
MUHAMMAD. *Carpet with Hunting Scene* (detail). Iran, 1530–40.
Silk; knotted pile, with discontinuous supplementary
metallic wefts, 15 ft. 9 in. x 8 ft. 4 in. (4.8 x 2.55 m).

Candlestick.
Egypt, 1342 (Mamlūk period). Hammered brass inlaid
with silver and gold, height: 14 in. (35.6 cm).

ART OF THE AMERICAS

In 1870 the first object acquired by the newly founded Museum of Fine Arts was a nineteenth-century American painting. Less than a decade later, the Museum received almost fifty ancient Peruvian weavings—intricate, rare, and beautiful textiles of profound sacred and secular meaning. And so the American collections were begun.

Bostonians—citizens of a historic city with a deep respect for tradition—have been fundamental in shaping the character and quality of American art at the Museum. Not surprisingly, the collections are especially rich in the arts of early New England. More than one hundred portraits by John Singleton Copley and Gilbert Stuart preserve the proud faces of early America's most notable political figures—Samuel Adams, Paul Revere (page 124), John Hancock, General Henry Knox, and George Washington (page 126), to name a few. Equally strong are the holdings of furniture, needlework, and silver from the Colonial and early national periods. In the galleries, for example, one can admire both Copley's celebrated portrait of fellow Bostonian Paul Revere and an unsurpassed collection of Revere silver, including the Liberty Bowl (page 127), a national treasure that commemorates Boston's assertion of basic human rights in the years just before the Revolution.

Among period settings are three rooms from Oak Hill, built in 1800–1801 for the daughter of America's first millionaire, Elias Hasket Derby, of Salem, Massachusetts. The rooms have been restored with scrupulous accuracy and care, and contain many original furnishings (page 135).

One of the Museum's greatest benefactors was Maxim Karolik, a flamboyant Russian émigré who saw America as "the only hope and promised land to all mankind." Karolik married socially prominent Bostonian Martha Codman in 1928; working closely with Museum curators, the Karoliks acquired and donated major collections of eighteenth-century furniture, nineteenth-century watercolors and drawings, and paintings from the then-neglected period from 1815 to 1875. Maxim Karolik rediscovered many forgotten painters, notably Martin Johnson Heade and Fitz Hugh Lane, whose serene and lyrical images of the New England coast are now among the most sought-after American paintings (pages 150 and 139).

The Karolik Collection also includes unusually vital and original works by untrained artists. An outstanding example is a quilt—worked with images from the Bible, local legends, and astronomical occurrences—that was created about 1895 by Harriet Powers, an African-American woman living in Georgia (page 137).

The Museum has nearly two thousand American watercolors, ranging from works by talented amateurs to the dazzling creations of Winslow Homer and John Singer Sargent (pages 156 and 145). Oil paintings by these foremost American artists include Homer's *The Fog Warning,* a classic image of the confrontation of man and nature (page 157), and Sargent's memorable *The Daughters of Edward D. Boit* (page 153), which was given to the Museum by the four sitters in 1919.

The Museum is continually striving to expand and enrich its American collections, with particular attention to the arts of indigenous populations of the Americas, contemporary decorative arts, and objects that were made in regions other than the cities of the eastern United States. Through these efforts, the collection has come to reflect more broadly the ethnic and cultural influences that have shaped the Americas and their art.

ON PAGE 108: *Mantle with Design of Ritual Impersonators* (detail).
Peru, Paracas, c. A.D. 50–100.
Camelid fiber, plain weave, embroidered with camelid fiber,
39¾ x 96⅛ in. (101 x 244.3 cm).

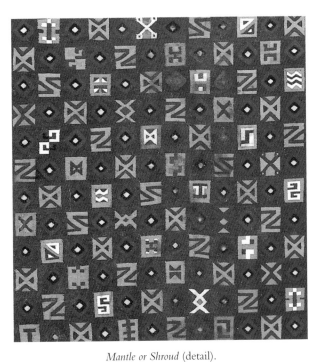

Mantle or Shroud (detail).
Peru, Neo-Inca culture, c. 1550.
Camelid fiber and cotton, tapestry weave, with
overstitched edging, 46⅞ x 67⅜ in. (119 x 171 cm).

Four-Cornered Hat.
Peru, Wari culture, c. 500–800.
Camelid fiber, knotted looping with supplementary
cut pile, height: 4½ in. (11.4 cm).

Cylinder Vase Depicting Itzamna and the Hero Twins.
Maya, Mexico, Central Campeche, 593–830.
Ceramic with orange, red, white, and black slip decoration
on cream slip ground, 8 x 6¾ in. (20.3 x 17.1 cm).

Plate Depicting the Resurrection of Hun Hunahpu.
Maya, Guatemala, Petén region, 700–900.
Ceramic with black and red slip decoration on
cream slip ground, diameter: 12¼ in. (31.1 cm).

Mask.
Olmec, Veracruz, c. 1150–550 B.C. (Middle Preclassic).
Gray jadeite with black inclusions,
height: 8½ inches (21.6 cm).

Zoomorphic Effigy.
New Mexico, 1100–1225 (Mogollon, Tularosa phase).
Gray earthenware with white and black slip,
10 x 7½ x 6¼ in. (25.4 x 19.1 x 15.9 cm).

FREAKE-GIBBS PAINTER.
Portrait of Robert Gibbs at Four and a Half Years, 1670.
Oil on canvas, 40⅛ x 33 in. (101.9 x 83.8 cm).

ATTRIBUTED TO THE SYMONDS SHOP.
Joined Chest with Drawer. Salem, Massachusetts, 1660–1700.
Oak, maple, walnut, and cedar,
28⅞ x 46 x 20¾ in. (73.3 x 116.8 x 52.7 cm).

Leather Great Chair. Boston, 1665–80.
Oak and maple, with original leather upholstery,
38 x 23⅝ x 16⅜ in. (96.5 x 61 x 41.6 cm).

JOHN CONEY (1655–1722).
Sugar Box. Boston, c. 1680–90.
Silver, 4¹³⁄₁₆ x 6 x 7¾ in. (12.2 x 15.2 x 19.8 cm).

ATTRIBUTED TO EUNICE BOURNE (1732–1773/81).
Chimneypiece pictorial embroidery known as
The Fishing Lady and Boston Common, c. 1748.
Linen, plain weave; embroidered with wool, silk, and
metallic threads, and beads, 20⅞ x 43¾ in. (53 x 111 cm).

JOSEPH BLACKBURN (active 1753–63).
Isaac Winslow and His Family, 1755.
Oil on canvas, 54½ x 79¼ in. (138.4 x 201.3 cm).

John Singleton Copley (1738–1815).
Paul Revere, 1768.
Oil on canvas, 35⅛ x 28½ in. (89.2 x 72.4 cm).

PAUL REVERE II (1735–1818).
Teapot. Boston, c. 1760–65. Silver,
height: 5⅞ in. (14.9 cm), diameter of base: 3¼ in. (8.3 cm).

GILBERT STUART (1755–1828).
George Washington, 1796.
Oil on canvas, 47¾ x 37 in. (121.3 x 94 cm).

PAUL REVERE II (1735–1818).
Sons of Liberty Bowl. Boston, 1768.
Silver, height: 5½ in. (14 cm), diameter of lip: 11 in. (28 cm).

Desk and Bookcase. Salem, Massachusetts, 1760–80.
Mahogany and white pine,
99¾ x 46½ x 25 in. (253.4 x 118.1 x 63.5 cm).

DANIEL CHRISTIAN FUETER (1720–1785).
Bread Basket. New York, c. 1754–69. Silver,
10¹¹⁄₁₆ x 14⅞ in. (27.1 x 37.8 cm).

JOHN COGSWELL (1738–1818).
Chest-on-Chest. Boston, 1782. Mahogany and white pine,
89½ x 43½ x 23½ in. (227.3 x 110.5 x 59.7 cm).

DESIGN AND CARVING ATTRIBUTED TO
SAMUEL MCINTIRE (1757–1811). *Chest-on-Chest.*
Salem, Massachusetts, 1796. Mahogany veneer on white pine,
102½ x 46¾ x 23 in. (260.4 x 118.7 x 58.4 cm).

WASHINGTON ALLSTON (1779–1843).
Moonlit Landscape, 1819.
Oil on canvas, 24 x 35 in. (61 x 88.9 cm).

JOHN SINGLETON COPLEY (1738–1815).
Watson and the Shark, 1778.
Oil on canvas, 72¼ x 90⅜ in. (183.5 x 229.6 cm).

THOMAS SEYMOUR (1771–1843), WITH PAINTED DECORATION
BY JOHN RITTO PENNIMAN (1783–1837).
Commode. Boston, 1809. Mahogany, satinwood, and other
woods, 41½ x 50 x 24½ in. (105.4 x 127 x 62.2 cm).

Parlor of Oak Hill, built 1800–1801,
in Danvers, Massachusetts,
for Elizabeth Derby West.

THOMAS COLE (1801–1848).
Expulsion from the Garden of Eden, c. 1827–28.
Oil on canvas, 39 x 54 in. (99 x 137.2 cm).

HARRIET POWERS (1837–1911).
Pictorial Quilt, c. 1895–98. Cotton; printed, pieced, appliquéd,
and embroidered with cotton, silk, and metallic threads,
68⅞ x 105⅛ in. (175 x 267 cm).

H. E. BOUCHER MANUFACTURING COMPANY.
Flying Cloud, clipper ship model, 1916. Polychromed pine,
mahogany, boxwood, cambric, silk, paper, glass, brass, and steel,
38 x 24 x 62 in. (96.5 x 61 x 157.5 cm).

FITZ HUGH LANE (1804–1865).
Boston Harbor, c. 1855–58.
Oil on canvas, 26¼ x 32 in. (66.8 x 106.7 cm).

WILLIAM SIDNEY MOUNT (1807–1868).
The Bone Player, 1856.
Oil on canvas, 36⅛ x 29⅛ in. (91.8 x 74 cm).

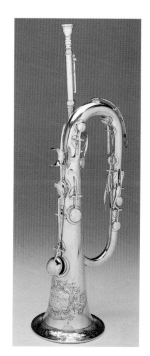

ELBRIDGE G. WRIGHT (1811–1871).
Keyed Bugle. Boston, c. 1854.
Silver, 17½ x 7½ x 4⅛ in. (44.5 x 19 x 10.4 cm).

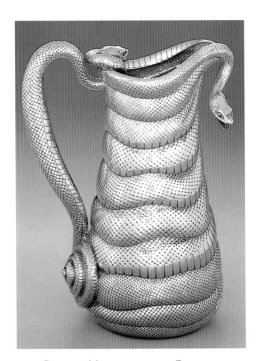

GORHAM MANUFACTURING COMPANY.
Snake Pitcher. Providence, Rhode Island, c. 1885.
Silver, 10 x 7¼ x 4½ in. (25.4 x 18.4 x 11.4 cm).

IGNATIUS LUTZ (active 1844–60).
Sideboard. Philadelphia, c. 1850–60. Oak, yellow-poplar,
and marble, 94 x 74 x 25 in. (238.8 x 188 x 64 cm).

WINSLOW HOMER (1836–1910).
Boys in a Pasture, 1874.
Oil on canvas, 15¼ x 22½ in. (38.7 x 57 cm).

JOHN SINGER SARGENT (1856–1925).
Simplon Pass: The Lesson, 1911.
Watercolor on paper, 15 x 18¼ in. (38.1 x 46.4 cm).

CHILDE HASSAM (1859–1935).
Boston Common at Twilight, 1885–86.
Oil on canvas, 42 x 60 in. (106.7 x 152.4 cm).

JOHN J. STEVENS (1824–1902).
Walking Dress. Boston, c. 1874–75.
Silk with knotted-net trim and tassles.

JOHN NEAGLE (1796–1860).
Pat Lyon at the Forge, 1826–27.
Oil on canvas, 93 x 68 in. (236.1 x 172.6 cm).

THOMAS EAKINS (1844–1916).
The Dean's Roll Call, 1899.
Oil on canvas, 84 x 42 in. (213.4 x 106.7 cm).

MARTIN JOHNSON HEADE (1819–1904).
Approaching Storm: Beach Near Newport, 1860s.
Oil on canvas, 28 x 58¼ in. (71.1 x 147.9 cm).

ALBERT BIERSTADT (1830–1902).
Wreck of the "Ancon" in Loring Bay, Alaska, 1889. Oil on paper
mounted on Masonite, 14⅛ x 19¾ in. (35.9 x 50.2 cm).

ERASTUS SALISBURY FIELD (1805–1900).
Joseph Moore and His Family, 1839.
Oil on canvas, 82¾ x 93¼ in. (210.2 x 238.1 cm).

John Singer Sargent (1856–1925).
The Daughters of Edward D. Boit, 1882.
Oil on canvas, 87 x 87 in. (221 x 221 cm).

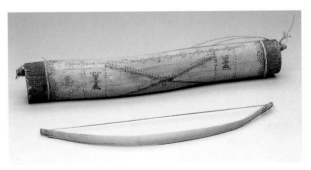

Fiddle and Bow. White Mountain Apache people, Arizona, 19th century. Mescal stalk and horsehair, 13⅜ x 2 in. (34 x 5 cm).

Raven Rattle. Kwakiutl people, British Columbia,
19th century. Polychrome wood,
12¼ x 3¾ x 3¼ in. (31 x 9.5 x 8.1 cm).

WINSLOW HOMER (1836–1910).
The Blue Boat, 1892.
Watercolor on paper, 15⅛ x 21½ in. (38.4 x 54.6 cm).

WINSLOW HOMER (1836–1910).
The Fog Warning, 1885.
Oil on canvas, 30 x 47⅞ in. (76.2 x 121.6 cm).

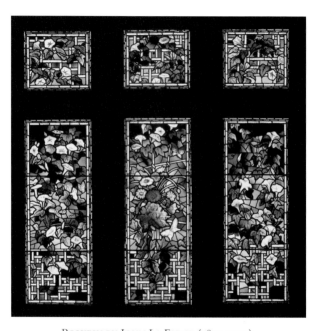

POSSIBLY BY JOHN LA FARGE (1835–1910).
Morning Glories. Window from William Watts Sherman house,
Newport, Rhode Island, 1877–78.
158   Stained glass, 86½ x 72 in. (220 x 183 cm).

John Frederick Peto (1854–1907).
The Poor Man's Store, 1885.
Oil on canvas and panel, 35½ x 25⅝ in. (90.2 x 65.1 cm).

ELIHU VEDDER (1836–1923).
The Questioner of the Sphinx, 1863.
Oil on canvas, 36¼ x 42¼ in. (92.1 x 107.3 cm).

Thomas Crawford (1811/13?–1857).
Orpheus and Cerberus, 1843.
Marble, height: 67½ in. (171.45 cm).

EUROPEAN ART

European art at the Museum is represented by paintings, sculpture, musical instruments, works on paper, a wide range of decorative objects, and textiles.

When the Museum was founded, in 1870, Boston was the center of the American textile industry; the new Museum began immediately to acquire textiles that would provide manufacturers with superior examples of design. Today the textile collection is extensive. Among its primary European holdings are English and Continental embroideries, weavings, and laces; costumes (especially lavishly decorated eighteenth-century formal dress for men and women); and embroideries from Greece and the Greek islands. Superb tapestries from the great European weaving centers include a richly decorative hanging depicting vain Narcissus gazing ardently at his own reflection (page 175).

The Museum's remarkable collection of works on paper contains over three hundred thousand European and American prints, drawings, watercolors, illustrated books, and photographs. Many major artists are represented by work in more than one medium: the Albrecht Dürer holdings, for example, are rich in drawings, engravings (page 176), etchings, drypoints, and woodcuts. Like textiles, fragile works on paper are susceptible to the damaging effects of light and are therefore exhibited on a rotating basis.

Prints are often acquired in multiple impressions, giving scholars the opportunity to learn by comparison; this is invaluable in the case of artists like Rembrandt van Rijn, who was constantly experimenting. Rembrandt's prints and drawings complement such paintings by the master as the small, evocative image of a young artist confronting his easel (page 185).

Seventeenth-century Dutch paintings and Italian works of all periods are features of the comprehensive collection of European painting. Many of these works reflect pioneering Boston tastes. In 1893 Henry Lee Higginson, founder of the Boston Symphony Orchestra, donated Rogier van der Weyden's *Saint Luke Painting the Virgin and Child* (page 177), the first great Flemish picture to come to America. Similarly, the acute, expressive portrait of a Spanish monk became one of the first El Grecos in an American museum (page 182).

One-third of the Museum's European paintings are nineteenth-century French, including the world-famous Impressionist and Post-Impressionist masterworks illustrated in the next chapter. Most came into Boston private collections before 1900 and were given to the Museum by descendants of the original owners. In the mid-nineteenth century, artist and teacher William Morris Hunt was particularly influential in introducing French painting to Boston. Hunt was a student of Jean-François Millet, the revolutionary painter of peasant life; he bought Millet's powerful *The Sower* (page 209) from the artist for sixty dollars and sold it to Quincy Adams Shaw. Shaw became foremost among the enthusiastic Boston collectors of Millet's work and, in 1917, his heirs gave the Museum almost sixty paintings and pastels.

Sculpture and decorative arts from Europe include distinguished collections of medieval sculpture and metalwork, eighteenth-century French decorative arts and English porcelain, and French and English silver. Donatello's intimate and subtle marble relief, *Madonna of the Clouds* (page 174), is one of very few works in the United States by this master of the early Italian Renaissance. A European highlight of the musical instrument collection, which includes examples from around the world, is the magnificent English piano, decorated with Wedgwood cameos and exotic woods, that was apparently commissioned by a prime minister of Spain for his lover, the queen (page 195).

BARNA DA SIENA (active mid-14th century).
The Mystic Marriage of Saint Catherine, c. 1340.
Tempera on panel, design: 53⅛ x 42⅛ in. (134.8 x 107.1 cm).

DUCCIO DI BUONINSEGNA (active 1278–1319)
AND WORKSHOP. *The Crucifixion; The Redeemer with Angels;
Saint Nicholas; Saint Gregory,* c. 1310.
Tempera on panel, center: 24 x 15½ in. (60 x 39.5 cm).   167

Reliquary (Emly Shrine). Ireland, late 7th–early 8th century.
Champlevé enamel on bronze over yew wood with
gilt-bronze moldings and inlay of lead-tin alloy,
3⅝ x 4⅛ in. (9.2 x 10.5 cm).

Plaque with Three Worthies in the Fiery Furnace. Meuse,
(Maastricht?), 3d quarter of 12th century.
Champlevé enamel and gilding on copper,
height: 8³⁄₁₆ in. (20.8 cm).

Christ in Majesty with Symbols of the Four Evangelists;
The Apostles with Scenes from the Story of Cain and Abel;
and Scenes from the Life of Christ.
Spanish (Catalan), 12th century. Fresco secco transferred
to plaster and wood, height: 21 ft. 2 in. (6.45 m).

Tapestry with Wild Men and Moors (detail).
Upper Rhineland (probably Strasbourg), 1400–1440.
Linen and wool, tapestry weave,
3 ft. 3 in. x 15 ft. 10 in. (99 cm x 4.8 m).

MASTER OF THE AMSTERDAM CABINET.
Mother with Two Children and a Blank Shield.
German, c. 1470–1500.
Drypoint, 3¾ x 2⅞ in. (9.5 x 7.3 cm).

MASTER OF THE AMSTERDAM CABINET.
Bearded Man with a Blank Shield.
German, c. 1470–1500.
Drypoint, 3¾ x 2⅞ in. (9.5 x 7.3 cm).

DONATELLO (1386–1466).
Madonna of the Clouds, c. 1425–30.
Marble, 13 x 12⅝ in. (33.1 x 32 cm).

Narcissus. French or the Franco-Flemish territories,
late 15th or early 16th century. Wool and silk, tapestry weave,
111 x 122½ in. (282 x 311 cm).

ALBRECHT DÜRER (1471–1528).
Saint Jerome in His Study, 1514.
Engraving, 9¾ x 7½ in. (24.8 x 19.1 cm).

ROGIER VAN DER WEYDEN (c. 1400–1464).
Saint Luke Painting the Virgin and Child, c. 1435–40.
Oil and tempera on panel,
design: 53⅛ x 42⅝ in. (135 x 108.2 cm).

ROSSO FIORENTINO (1496–1540).
The Dead Christ with Angels, c. 1524–27.
Oil on panel, 52½ x 41 in. (133.5 x 104.1 cm).

CARLO CRIVELLI (active 1457–95).
Lamentation over the Dead Christ, 1485.
Tempera on panel, 34¾ x 20⅞ in. (86.6 x 51.1 cm).

LORENZO DI CREDI (1459?–1537).
Head of a Youth, c. 1500. Silverpoint heightened with white
on gray paper, 8³⁄₁₆ x 7⅝ in. (20.8 x 19.4 cm.)

GIAMBOLOGNA (1529–1608).
Architecture. Florence, late 16th century.
Bronze, height: 14¼ in. (36.1 cm).

EL GRECO (1541–1614).
Fray Hortensio Félix Paravicino, 1609.
Oil on canvas, 44⅛ x 33⅞ in. (112 x 86.1 cm).

REMBRANDT VAN RIJN (1606–1669).
Portrait of a Woman Wearing a Gold Chain, 1634.
Oil on panel, 27⅜ x 20⅞ in. (69.5 x 53 cm).

REMBRANDT VAN RIJN (1606–1669).
Watchdog in His Kennel, c. 1638.
Pen and brown ink on paper, 5⅝ x 6⅝ in. (14.4 x 16.8 cm).

REMBRANDT VAN RIJN (1606–1669).
Artist in His Studio, c. 1627/28.
Oil on panel, 9¾ x 12½ in. (24.8 x 31.7 cm).

Rembrandt van Rijn (1606–1669).
Abraham Caressing Isaac, c. 1637.
Copper etching plate, 4⅝ x 3½ in. (11.6 x 8.9 cm).

Diego Rodríquez de Silva y Velázquez (1599–1660).
Don Baltasar Carlos with a Dwarf, 1632.
Oil on canvas, 50⅜ x 40⅛ in. (128.1 x 102 cm).

NICOLAS POUSSIN (1594–1665).
Mars and Venus, c. 1627–29.
Oil on canvas, 61 x 84⅛ in. (154.9 x 213.5 cm).

PETER PAUL RUBENS (1577–1640).
The Sacrifice of the Old Covenant, c. 1626.
Oil on panel, 27¾ x 34½ in. (70.8 x 87.6 cm).

ALEXANDER VOBOAM I (active 1652–80).
Guitar. Paris, 1680. Ebony and spruce body,
36⅛ x 9⅞ x 3⅝ in. (91.9 x 25 x 9.3 cm).

DIRCK VAN BABUREN (1590/95–1624).
The Procuress, 1622.
Oil on canvas, 40 x 42⅜ in. (101.5 x 107.6 cm).

JEAN-BAPTISTE-SIMÉON CHARDIN (1699–1779).
Kitchen Table, 1755.
Oil on canvas, 15⅝ x 18¾ in. (39.8 x 47.5 cm).

LUIS MELÉNDEZ (1716–1780).
Still Life with Bread, Ham, Cheese, and Vegetables, c. 1770.
Oil on canvas, 24⅜ x 33½ in. (62 x 85.2 cm).

JEAN-FERDINAND SCHWERDFEGER (1739–1818).
Fall Front Secretary. Paris, 1788.
Mahogany, oak, gilt bronze, brass, and white marble,
55¼ x 33¼ x 13½ in. (140.3 x 84.4 x 34.2 cm).

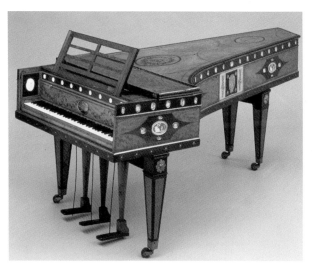

JOHN BROADWOOD AND SON,
WITH CASE DECORATION BY THOMAS SHERATON.
Grand Piano. London, 1796. Veneered case of satinwood,
tulipwood, and purpleheart with Wedgwood cameos and
medallions, 97⅞ x 43⅞ x 35⅞ in. (248.7 x 111.5 x 91.2 cm). 195

WILLIAM KENT (1685–1748),
EXECUTED BY BALTHASAR FRIEDRICH BEHRENS (1701–1760).
Chandelier. Hannover, Germany, 1736.
Silver, 46½ x 37½ in. (118.1 x 95.2 cm).

ATTRIBUTED TO PIERRE-PHILIPPE THOMIRE (1751–1843).
Andiron (one of a pair). Paris, c. 1785.
Gilt and chased bronze, 19 x 18 in. (48.3 x 45.7 cm).

FRANÇOIS-THOMAS GERMAIN (1726–1791).
Sauceboat and Stand (one of a pair). Paris, 1757–58.
Silver, 5⅞ x 15¼ in. (14.8 x 38.8 cm).

CLAUDE MICHEL, CALLED CLODION (1738–1814).
The Deluge, 1800.
Terra-cotta, height: 21 in. (53.3 cm).

SÈVRES FACTORY.
Pair of Pots-Pourris in the Form of Snail Shells.
France, c. 1763–68. Soft-paste porcelain,
5⅛ x 6⅜ in. (13.1 x 16.3 cm).

CHELSEA FACTORY.
Covered Tureen in the Form of Hen and Chicks and Stand.
England, c. 1755. Soft-paste porcelain,
10 x 15 in. (25.4 x 38.1 cm).

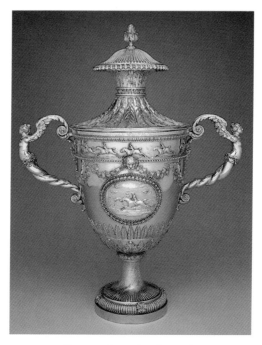

ROBERT ADAM (1728–1792),
MARKED BY DANIEL SMITH AND ROBERT SHARP.
Richmond Race Cup. London, 1764.
Gilt silver, 19¼ x 15⅝ in. (48.9 x 39.7 cm).

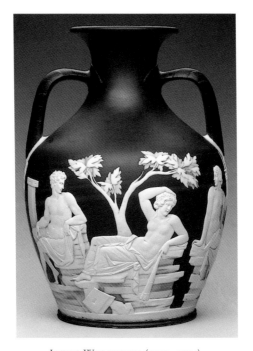

JOSIAH WEDGWOOD (1730–1795).
Copy of the Portland Vase. Wedgwood, England,
c. 1790. Jasperware (colored stoneware),
height: 10 in. (25.4 cm), diameter: 8½ in. (21.5 cm).

ELISABETH VIGÉE-LE RUN (1755–1842).
Portrait of a Young Woman, c. 1797.
Oil on canvas, 32⅜ x 27¾ in. (82.2 x 70.5 cm).

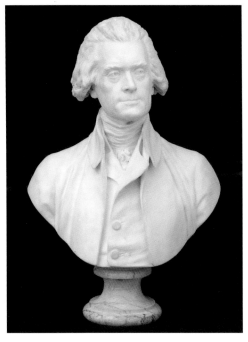

JEAN-ANTOINE HOUDON (1741–1828).
Bust of Thomas Jefferson, 1789.
Marble, height: 26¾ in. (68 cm).

JOSEPH MALLORD WILLIAM TURNER (1775–1851).
*Slave Ship (Slavers Throwing Overboard the Dead and Dying,
Typhoon Coming On)*, 1840. Oil on canvas,
35¾ x 48¼ in. (90.8 x 122.6 cm).

GIOVANNI ANTONIO CANAL, CALLED CANALETTO (1697–1768).
San Giorgio Maggiore: From the Bacino di San Marco, c. 1730.
Oil on canvas, 18⅝ x 24⅞ in. (46.5 x 63.3 cm).

Francisco Goya (1746–1828).
Colossus, 1818.
Aquatint, 11¼ x 8¼ in. (28.5 x 21 cm).

Jean-François Millet (1814–1875).
The Sower, 1850.
Oil on canvas, 40 x 32½ in. (101.6 x 82.6 cm).

JEAN-FRANÇOIS MILLET (1814–1875).
Noonday Rest, 1866. Pastel and black Conté crayon on paper,
11⅜ x 16½ in. (28.8 x 42 cm).

JEAN-FRANÇOIS MILLET (1814–1875).
Potato Planters, 1861–62.
Oil on canvas, 32½ x 39⅞ in. (82.5 x 101.3 cm).

WILLIAM MORRIS (1834–1896).
"Tulip" Design Furnishing Fabric,
printed for Morris & Company by Thomas Wardle & Co.,
1875. Block-printed cotton, 27 x 60¼ in. (68.5 x 153 cm).

Frederick H. Evans (1853–1943).
In the Attics, Kelmscott Manor, 1896.
Platinum print, 6¹⁄₁₆ x 7¹⁵⁄₁₆ in. (15.2 x 20.2 cm).

GUSTAVE COURBET (1819–1877).
The Quarry, 1856.
Oil on canvas, 82¾ x 72¼ in. (210.2 x 183.5 cm).

JEAN-LÉON GÉRÔME (1824–1904).
L'Eminence Grise, 1873.
Oil on canvas, 27 x 39¾ in. (68.5 x 101 cm).

EUGÈNE DELACROIX (1798–1863).
Lion Hunt, 1858.
Oil on canvas, 36⅛ x 46¼ in. (91.7 x 117.5 cm).

EUGÈNE DELACROIX (1798–1863).
The Entombment of Christ, 1848.
Oil on canvas, 64 x 52 in. (162.6 x 132.1 cm).

Frederick Leighton (1830–1896).
Painter's Honeymoon, c. 1864.
Oil on canvas, 32⅞ x 30¼ in. (83.5 x 76.8 cm).

DANTE GABRIEL ROSSETTI (1828–1882).
Lips That Have Been Kissed, 1859.
Oil on panel, 12⅝ x 10⅝ in. (32.2 x 27.1 cm).

EDVARD MUNCH (1863–1944).
Summer Night's Dream (The Voice), 1893.
Oil on canvas, 34⅝ x 42½ in. (87.8 x 108 cm).

EDVARD MUNCH (1863–1944).
Melancholy, 1896.
Color woodcut on paper, 14⅞ x 17⅞ in. (37.8 x 45.4 cm).

IMPRESSIONISM AND POST-IMPRESSIONISM

Claude Monet's first museum-sponsored exhibition any-
where was held at the Museum of Fine Arts in 1911. He
had been Boston's favorite artist since the late 1880s,
when local painter Lilla Cabot Perry, who had worked
with Monet at Giverny, began to buy his paintings and
encourage her friends to do the same. In the generous
and public-spirited Boston tradition, many of these early
collectors or their heirs have presented their beloved
Monets to the Museum, which now holds the finest collection outside of Paris. Thirty-five paintings spanning
Monet's career range from the seascapes and woodland
scenes of the 1860s to his late, strikingly modern studies
of water lilies on the shifting surface of the pond at
Giverny (at left and page 243). Many of Monet's most
free and brilliant Impressionist landscapes are in the collection, as well as multiple examples of his famous grainstacks,
Rouen Cathedral (pages 240 and 241), and other series paintings of the 1890s.

Paintings by the other Impressionists and the Post-
Impressionists were almost equally admired in Boston and
as generously given. Robert Treat Paine II, for example,
presented the Museum with three extraordinary portraits: Edgar Degas's painting of his sister and her husband,

in which character and relationship are subtly revealed through pose, gesture, and expression (page 229); Paul Cézanne's monumental and complex image of his wife-to-be seated in their Paris apartment (page 254); and Vincent van Gogh's vital and expressive portrait of his friend Joseph Roulin, postmaster of the provincial town of Arles in the south of France (page 255).

The Museum's collection of French Impressionist and Post-Impressionist painting—one of the richest and most comprehensive in America—includes almost twenty works by Pierre-Auguste Renoir, notably the radiant, joyous *Dance at Bougival* (page 235); fifteen by Degas; five by Camille Pissarro; and numerous works by other painters. There are also prints and drawings by many of these artists, notably Edouard Manet, Degas, Paul Gauguin, Henri de Toulouse-Lautrec, and the American Impressionist Mary Cassatt, who spent her career in France. It was Cassatt who prompted the first two purchases by Bostonians of Manet paintings. Both are now at the Museum: *Street Singer*, in which Manet challenged the artistic establishment by painting a humble subject on a heroic scale (page 230), and *Execution of the Emperor Maximilian*, which documents the artist's outrage at the death of the Austrian-born ruler of Mexico (page 231).

Perhaps the most remarkable of the Museum's Post-Impressionist paintings is Gauguin's *Where Do We Come*

From? What Are We? Where Are We Going? (page 253). This giant canvas, with its mysterious figures and deep, warm colors, was painted in Tahiti near the end of the artist's life; Gauguin considered it his masterpiece and the culmination of his career.

It is interesting to compare the work of American followers of the Impressionists, many of them Bostonians, with the French paintings. Childe Hassam (pages 146 and 232) was typical of many American painters of the time: when he went to Paris in 1886, he completely abandoned his dark, atmospheric Boston style in favor of the light, color, and lively brushwork of Impressionism.

EDGAR DEGAS (1834–1917).
The Little Dancer, original model 1878–81, cast c. 1921.
Bronze, gauze, and satin, height: 38¼ in. (97.1 cm).

EDGAR DEGAS (1834–1917).
The Violinist, c. 1879. Black and white chalk on
blue-gray paper, 16½ x 11¾ in. (41.9 x 29.8 cm).

EDGAR DEGAS (1834–1917).
Self-Portrait, 1857. Etching and drypoint on paper,
9⅛ x 5⅝ in. (23.2 x 14.2 cm).

EDGAR DEGAS (1834–1917).
Edmondo and Thérèse Morbilli, 1867.
Oil on canvas, 45⅞ x 34¾ in. (116.5 x 88.3 cm).

EDOUARD MANET (1832–1883).
Street Singer, 1862.
Oil on canvas, 67⅜ x 41⅝ in. (171.3 x 105.8 cm).

EDOUARD MANET (1832–1883).
Execution of the Emperor Maximilian, 1867.
Oil on canvas, 77½ x 102¼ in. (196 x 259.8 cm).

CHILDE HASSAM (1859–1935).
Grand Prix Day, 1887.
Oil on canvas, 24⅛ x 31 in. (61.3 x 78.7 cm).

EDGAR DEGAS (1834–1917).
Carriage at the Races, 1869.
Oil on canvas, 14⅜ x 22 in. (36.5 x 55.9 cm).

PIERRE-AUGUSTE RENOIR (1841–1919).
The Seine at Chatou, c. 1881.
Oil on canvas, 28⅞ x 36⅜ in. (73.5 x 92.5 cm).

PIERRE-AUGUSTE RENOIR (1841–1919).
Dance at Bougival, 1883.
Oil on canvas, 71⅝ x 38⅝ in. (181.8 x 98.1 cm).

FRANK BENSON (1862–1951).
Calm Morning, 1904.
Oil on canvas, 44⅜ x 36⅛ in. (112.7 x 91.8 cm).

CLAUDE MONET (1840–1926).
Camille Monet and a Child in the Artist's Garden in Argenteuil,
1875. Oil on canvas, 21¾ x 25½ in. (55.3 x 64.7 cm).

CAMILLE PISSARRO (1830–1903).
Sunlight on the Road, Pontoise, 1874.
Oil on canvas, 20⅝ x 32⅛ in. (52.3 x 81.5 cm).

PAUL CÉZANNE (1839–1906).
Turn in the Road, c. 1879–82.
Oil on canvas, 23⅞ x 28⅞ in. (60.5 x 73.5 cm).

CLAUDE MONET (1840–1926).
Grainstack (Sunset), 1891.
Oil on canvas, 28⅞ x 36½ in. (73.3 x 92.6 cm).

CLAUDE MONET (1840–1926).
Rouen Cathedral Facade and Tour d'Albane (Morning Effect),
1894. Oil on canvas, 41¾ x 29⅛ in. (106.1 x 73.9 cm).

PIERRE-AUGUSTE RENOIR (1841–1919).
Mixed Flowers in an Earthenware Pot, 1869. Oil on paperboard
mounted on canvas, 25½ x 21⅜ in. (64.9 x 54.2 cm).

CLAUDE MONET (1840–1926).
Water Lilies (II), 1907.
Oil on canvas, 35⅛ x 36¾ in. (89.3 x 93.4 cm).

MARY CASSATT (1844–1926).
Five O'Clock Tea, c. 1880.
Oil on canvas, 25½ x 36½ in. (64.8 x 92.7 cm).

HENRI DE TOULOUSE-LAUTREC (1864–1901).
Le Divan Japonais, 1893.
Lithographic poster, 32 x 24½ in. (81.5 x 62.3 cm).

PAUL GAUGUIN (1848–1903).
Hail Mary, 1894.
Color monotype on paper, 8¾ x 5⅝ in. (22.2 x 14.2 cm).

MARY CASSATT (1844–1926).
The Letter, 1890. Color drypoint and aquatint on paper,
16 x 11½ in. (40.6 x 29.2 cm).

MAURICE PRENDERGAST (1859–1924).
Umbrellas in the Rain, 1899.
Watercolor on paper, 13⅝ x 20½ in. (34.6 x 52.1 cm).

JOHN SINGER SARGENT (1856–1925).
Corfu: Lights and Shadows, 1909.
Watercolor on paper, 15¾ x 20⅞ in. (40 x 53 cm).

GUSTAVE CAILLEBOTTE (1848–1894).
Fruit Displayed on a Stand, c. 1881–82.
Oil on canvas, 30⅛ x 39⅝ in. (76.5 x 100.5 cm).

PAUL GAUGUIN (1848–1903).
Flowers and a Bowl of Fruit on a Table, 1895. Oil on canvas
mounted on paperboard, 17 x 24¾ in. (43.1 x 62.9 cm).

Paul Gauguin (1848–1903).
Fall In Love, You Will Be Happy, 1889.
Polychromed linden wood, height: 47⅛ in. (119.6 cm).

PAUL GAUGUIN (1848–1903).
Where Do We Come From? What Are We?
Where Are We Going? (detail), 1897.
Oil on canvas, 4 ft. 7 in. x 12 ft. 4 in. (1.39 x 3.75 m).

PAUL CÉZANNE (1839–1906).
Madame Cézanne in a Red Armchair, 1877.
Oil on canvas, 28½ x 22 in. (72.5 x 56 cm).

VINCENT VAN GOGH (1853–1890).
Postman Joseph Roulin, 1888.
Oil on canvas, 32 x 25¾ in. (81.2 x 65.3 cm).

VINCENT VAN GOGH (1853–1890).
Houses at Auvers, 1890.
Oil on canvas, 29¾ x 24⅜ in. (75.5 x 61.8 cm).

WILLIAM GLACKENS (1870–1938).
Flying Kites, Montmartre, 1906.
Oil on canvas, 26 x 34¼ in. (66 x 87 cm).

TWENTIETH-CENTURY ART

The Museum is constantly expanding and strengthening its holdings of twentieth-century art. Many of the major figures from the first half of the century are well represented, often in more than one medium. For example, the collection contains sculptures and works on paper by Pablo Picasso as well as his important painting *Rape of the Sabine Women* (at left and page 287). This moving protest against the horrors of war was painted when the artist was eighty-two years old. Largely due to the generosity of discerning collector William H. Lane and his wife, Saundra, an entire gallery is devoted to early American modernists, including Stuart Davis (page 280), John Marin, Arthur Dove (page 282), Joseph Stella (page 281), and Charles Sheeler. Georgia O'Keeffe's delicate *White Rose with Larkspur* (page 273) was selected by the artist herself for the Museum of Fine Arts.

Other highlights are a fine group of German Expressionist paintings, works by Jackson Pollock (page 283) and other members of the postwar New York School, and nine canvases with luminous bands of poured color by Morris Louis (page 288). Works by Andy Warhol include *Red Disaster,* which addresses violence in America through the haunting repetition of a single motif (page 286). Some contemporary artists approach traditional media in new ways, as does Mark Tansey, whose monochromatic oil paintings suggest photographs and illustrations (page 306). Other works explore new media: Joseph Beuys's *Capri-Batterie* is one—a charming and provocative metaphor of the relationship between nature and technology (page 293).

"Please Be Seated" is a Museum program that acquires furniture by contemporary American makers to become both part of the permanent collection and seating for visitors throughout the galleries. It includes chairs, benches, and settees by Wendell Castle (page 297), George Nakashima, Tage Frid, and many others. Studio furniture by European makers—for example, Ron Arad's elegant, flowing chair of stainless-steel mesh (page 305)—is also being actively acquired, as are European and American decorative and functional objects in wood, metal, and ceramic. Hundreds of pieces of contemporary American ceramics and a strong group of turned wooden vessels have recently entered the collection.

Twentieth-century photography, exhibited on a rotating basis, ranges from a representative selection of early photographs to major holdings by such artists as Alfred Stieglitz (page 272) and Walker Evans and innovative contemporary work by Cindy Sherman, Robert Mapplethorpe (page 294), and William Wegman (page 303).

A relatively recent activity at the Museum has been the acquisition of early twentieth-century wooden sculpture from west Africa (pages 262 and 263). The promised gift of a major local collection will greatly enrich the Museum's holdings of African art, which include an excellent group of nineteenth-century musical instruments as well as the world-famous archaeological collections of the arts of ancient Egypt and Nubia.

Double Eket Mask. Nigeria, Ibibio people, c. 1890–1920.
Wood, paint, and vegetable fiber,
20⅝ x 11 in. (52.5 x 28 cm).

Mask (Deangle). Ivory Coast, Dan people, 20th century.
Wood, vegetable fiber, and shell,
height: 16½ in. (41.9 cm).

EUGÈNE ATGET (1857–1927).
Versailles, Park, 1902. Gold-toned albumen print,
7³⁄₁₆ x 8⁹⁄₁₆ in. (18.3 x 21.7 cm).

ALVIN LANGDON COBURN (1882–1966).
Yosemite Falls, c. 1911.
Gum platinum print, 16 x 12½ in. (40.6 x 31.8 cm).

Pablo Picasso (1881–1973).
Head of a Woman, 1909.
Bronze, height: 16½ in. (41.9 cm).

PABLO PICASSO (1881–1973).
Standing Figure, 1908.
Oil on canvas, 59⅛ x 39½ in. (150.3 x 100.3 cm).

ROBERT DELAUNAY (1885–1941).
St. Séverin, 1909.
Watercolor on paper, 19⅛ x 13⅝ in. (48.6 x 34.6 cm).

CHARLES DEMUTH (1883–1935).
In the Province (Roofs), 1920.
Watercolor on cardboard, 23¾ x 19⅞ in. (60.3 x 50.5 cm).

GEORGIA O'KEEFFE (1887–1986).
Red and Black, 1916.
Watercolor on paper, 11 13/16 x 8 13/16 in. (30 x 22.4 cm).

OSKAR KOKOSCHKA (1886–1980).
Illustration to *The Dreaming Boys,* 1917.
Color lithograph, 9⁹⁄₁₆ x 11⅝ in. (24.5 x 29.5 cm).

271

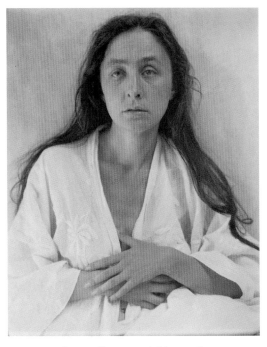

ALFRED STIEGLITZ (1864–1946).
A Portrait—Georgia O'Keeffe, 1918.
Palladium print, 9 3/16 x 7 1/2 in. (23.3 x 19.1 cm).

GEORGIA O'KEEFFE (1887–1986).
White Rose with Larkspur No. 2, 1927.
Oil on canvas, 40 x 30 in. (101.6 x 76.2 cm).

HENRI MATISSE (1869–1954).
Vase of Flowers, 1924.
Oil on canvas, 23⅞ x 29 in. (60.5 x 73.7 cm).

MARC CHAGALL (1887–1985).
Village Street, 1931–36.
Oil on canvas, 18⅛ x 15 in. (46. x 38 cm).

MARGUERITE ZORACH (1887–1968).
Central Panel from a Bedcover, 1925–28. Linen, plain weave,
embroidered with wool, 91⅛ x 71 in. (231.14 x 180.34 cm).

JEAN DUNAND (1877–1942).
Vase. France, c. 1925–30. Patinated metal overlaid with
red and green lacquer, silvered rim, height: 8⅞ in.
(22.5 cm), diameter: 11¾ in. (29.8 cm). 277

EDWARD HOPPER (1882–1967).
Lighthouse and Buildings, Portland Head, Cape Elizabeth, 1927.
Watercolor on paper, 13½ x 19½ in. (32.1 x 49.5 cm).

EDWARD HOPPER (1882–1967).
Room in Brooklyn, 1932.
Oil on canvas, 29 x 34 in. (73.6 x 86.3 cm).

STUART DAVIS (1892–1964).
Hot Still-scape for Six Colors—7th Ave. Style, 1940.
Oil on canvas, 36 x 44⅞ in. (91.4 x 114 cm).

JOSEPH STELLA (1877–1946).
Old Brooklyn Bridge, c. 1941.
Oil on canvas, 76¼ x 68¼ in. (193.7 x 173.4 cm).

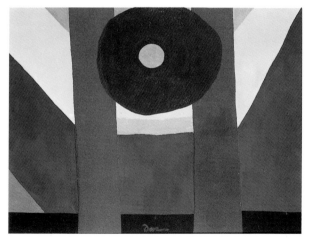

ARTHUR G. DOVE (1880–1946).
That Red One, 1944.
Tempera on canvas, 27 x 36 in. (68.6 x 91.4 cm).

Jackson Pollock (1912–1956).
Troubled Queen, 1946. Oil and enamel on canvas,
74 x 43½ in. (188 x 110.5 cm).

FRANZ KLINE (1910–1962).
Gray Abstraction, 1949.
Oil on beaverboard, 31½ x 41⅞ in. (80 x 106.4 cm).

HANS HOFMANN (1880–1966).
Twilight, 1957.
Oil on plywood, 48 x 36 in. (122 x 91.4 cm).

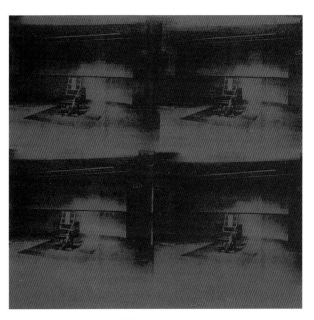

Andy Warhol (1928–1987).
Red Disaster, 1963 (detail).
Silkscreen ink on synthetic polymer paint on linen,
each panel: 93 x 80¼ in. (236.2 x 203.8 cm).

PABLO PICASSO (1881–1973).
Rape of the Sabine Women, 1963.
Oil on canvas, 76⅞ x 51⅝ in. (195.4 x 131 cm).

MORRIS LOUIS (1912–1962).
Delta Gamma, c̀. 1960. Acrylic resin (Magna) on canvas,
8 ft. 7 in. x 12 ft. 6 in. (2.62 x 3.82 m).

DAVID SMITH (1906–1965).
Cubi XVIII, 1964.
Polished stainless steel, height: 115¾ in. (294 cm).

JEAN DUBUFFET (1901–1985).
The Inquisitor, 1973. Epoxy, polyurethane, and paint,
34 x 23 x 13 in. (86.4 x 58.4 x 33 cm).

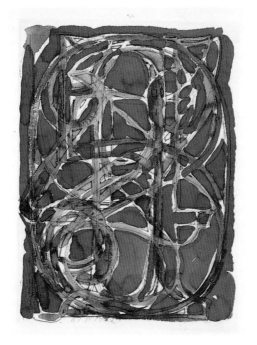

JASPER JOHNS (b. 1930).
0 Through 9, 1981. Wash drawing over etching on paper,
18 x 24 in. (45.7 x 61 cm).

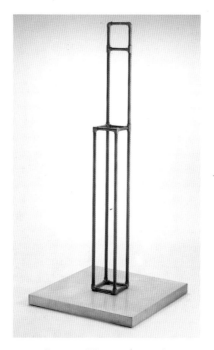

ROBERT WILSON (b. 1941).
Einstein Chair, 1976 design, 1985 edition.
Galvanized pipe, 89⅛ x 9⅞ in. (226.4 x 25.1 cm). Base:
metal-covered wood, 3 x 40 x 40 in. (7.6 x 101.6 x 101.6 cm).

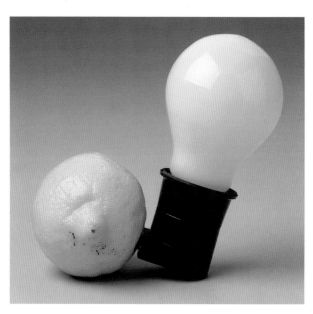

JOSEPH BEUYS (1921–1986).
Capri-Batterie, 1985. Light bulb, socket, and lemon,
7¼ x 7¼ x 6¹¹⁄₁₆ in. (18.4 x 18.4 x 17 cm).

ROBERT MAPPLETHORPE (1946–1989).
Ken Moody, 1984.
Unique Polaroid, 24 x 20 in. (61 x 50.8 cm).

FAITH RINGGOLD (b. 1930).
Dream 2: King and the Sisterhood, 1988. Acrylic on canvas,
pieced, dyed, and printed fabric, 96 x 60 in. (243.8 x 152.4 cm).

ALBERT PALEY (b. 1944).
Plant Stand. Rochester, New York, 1988–89.
Forged and fabricated mild steel, brass, and slate,
56½ x 25½ in. (143.5 x 54.8 cm).

WENDELL CASTLE (b. 1932).
Settee. Rochester, New York, 1979.
Cherry, 58 x 36 x 24 in. (147.3 x 91.4 x 61 cm).

LILLIAN SALVADORE (b. 1944).
Olla. Acoma, New Mexico, 1984.
Earthenware with white, black, and red slip,
height: 9 in. (22.9 cm.), diameter: 11¼ in. (28.6 cm).

ROB BUTLER (b. 1955).
Animal Bowl. Northeast, New York, 1990. Silver gilt,
height: 8½ in. (21.6 cm), diameter: 12½ in. (31.8 cm).

THOMAS HUCKER (b. 1955).
High Chest of Drawers, 1989. Black-lacquered plywood,
ebonized maple, aboya burl veneer, anodized aluminum, and
300   black brass, 75½ x 50½ x 21 in. (191.8 x 128.3 x 53.3 cm).

JUDY KENSLEY MCKIE (b. 1944).
Leopard Chest. Cambridge, Massachusetts, 1989.
Basswood, oil paint, and gilding,
33⅜ x 49⅞ x 18 in. (84.8 x 126.7 x 45.7 cm).

SCOTT PRIOR (b. 1949).
Nanny and Rose, 1983.
Oil on canvas, 66 x 58 in. (167.6 x 147.3 cm).

WILLIAM WEGMAN (b. 1943).
Intirely, 1990.
Unique Polaroid, 24 x 20 in. (61 x 50.8 cm).

ALESSANDRO MENDINI (b. 1931).
Poltrona di Proust. Milan, designed in 1978, made by Studio
Alchima, 1991. Carved and painted wood with painted
upholstery, 42½ x 40¾ x 35 in. (108 x 103.5 x 89 cm).

RON ARAD (b. 1951).
London Papardelle. London, 1992–93.
Stainless-steel mesh and mild steel,
41⅜ x 16 x 42¾ in. (105.1 x 40.6 x 108.5 cm).

MARK TANSEY (b. 1949).
The Enunciation, 1992.
Oil on canvas, 84 x 64 in. (213.4 x 162.6 cm).

DAVID BATES (b. 1952).
Magnolia, 1993.
Oil on canvas, 30 x 50 in. (76.2 x 127 cm).

DONOR INDEX

INDEX OF ILLUSTRATIONS

Editor: Mary Christian
Museum Editor: Peggy Hogan
Designer: Kevin Callahan
Production Editor: Meredith Wolf
Production Manager: Lou Bilka

First hardcover edition

15 14 13 12 11 10 9 8 7 6 5 4 3 2

Library of Congress Cataloging-in-Publication Data
Museum of Fine Arts, Boston.
    Treasures of the Museum of Fine Arts, Boston / introduction by
Malcolm Rogers : chapter introductions by Gilian Wohlauer.
        p. cm   "A tiny folio."
    Includes indexes.
    ISBN 0-7892-0506-8 (hc) / ISBN 0-7892-0146-1 (pb)
    1. Art—Massachusetts—Boston—Catalogs. 2. Museum of Fine Arts.
Boston—Catalogs. I. Rogers, Malcolm. II. Title.
N520-A77 1996
708-144'61—dc20   96-13377